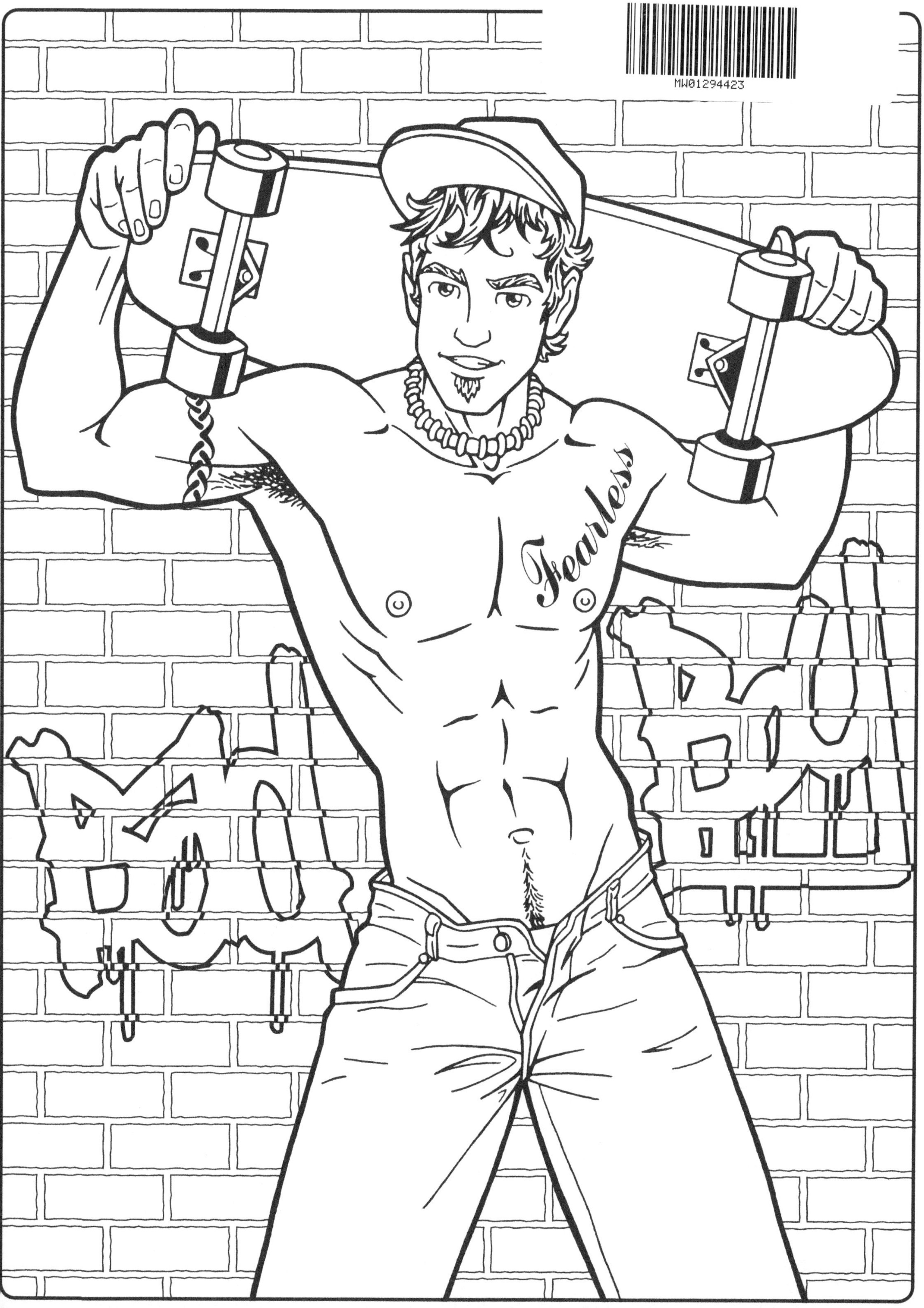
Fearless

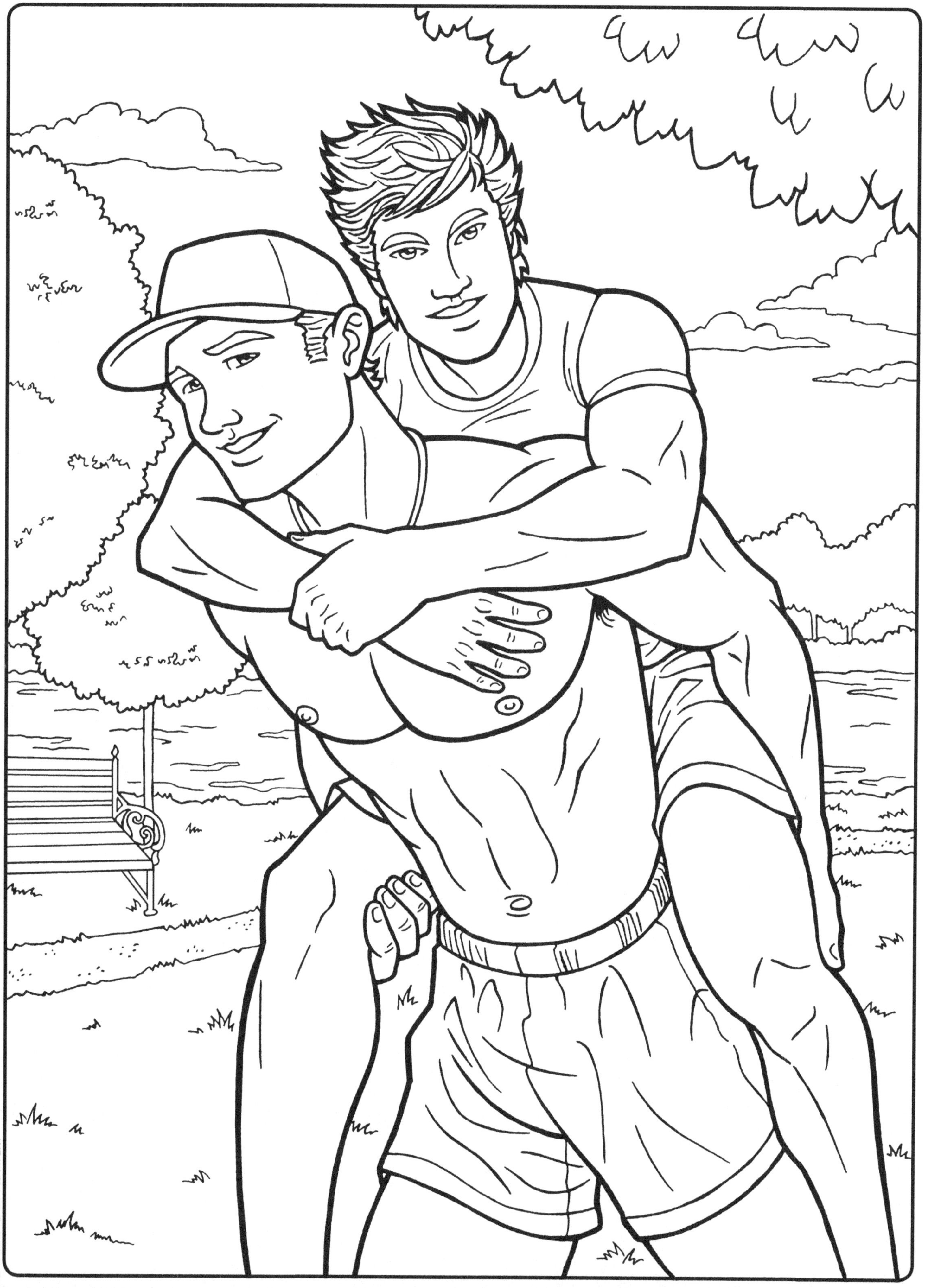

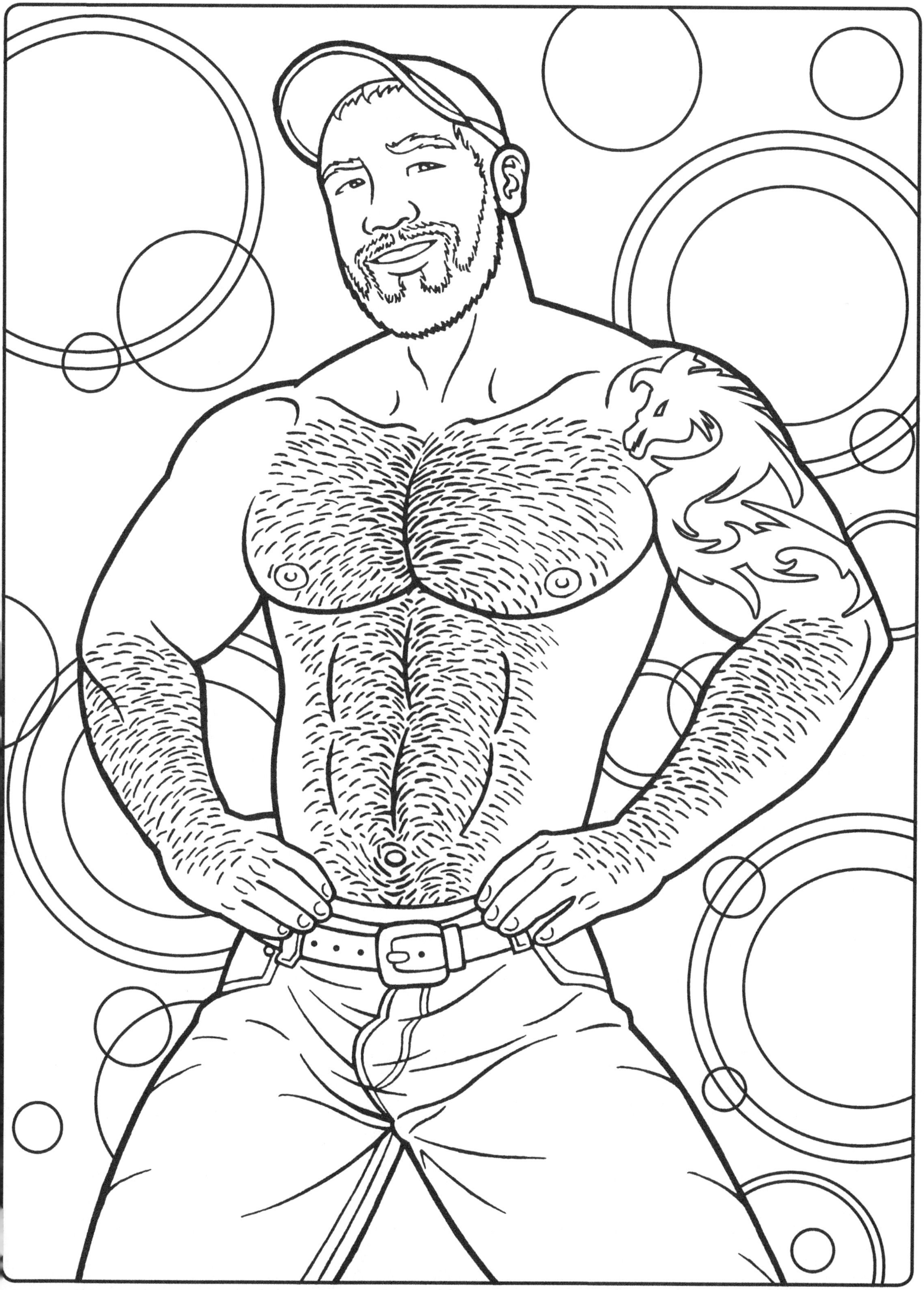

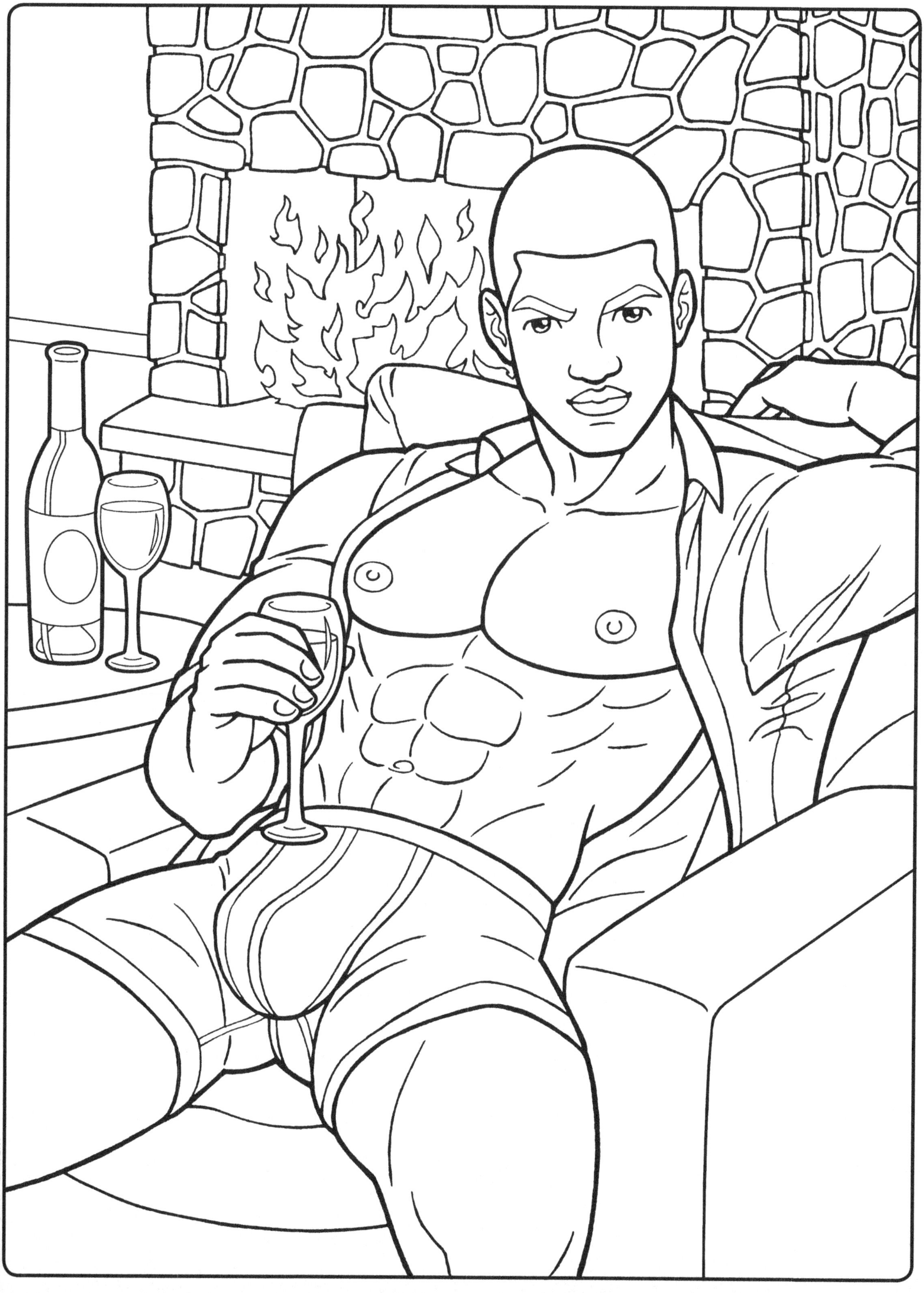

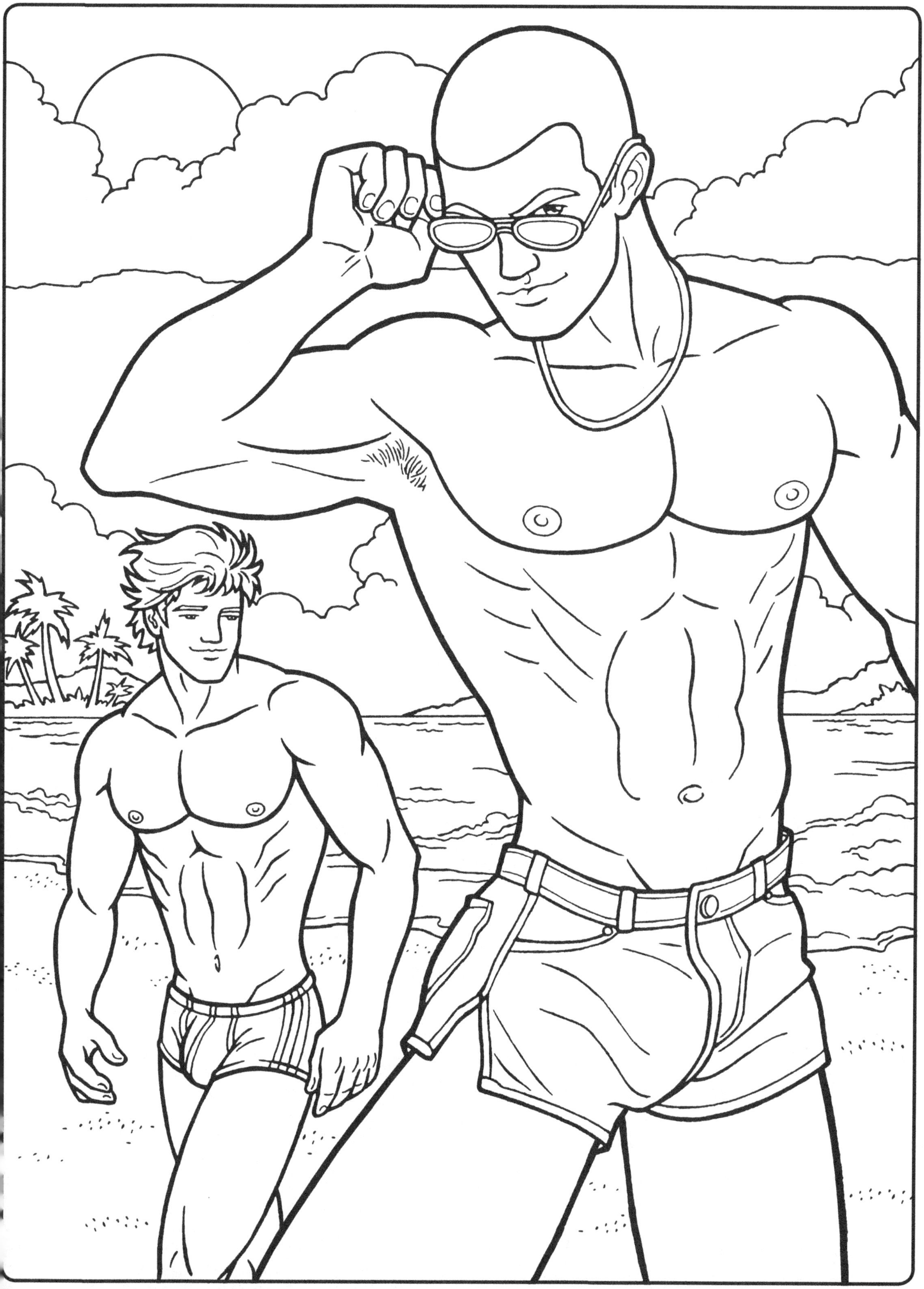

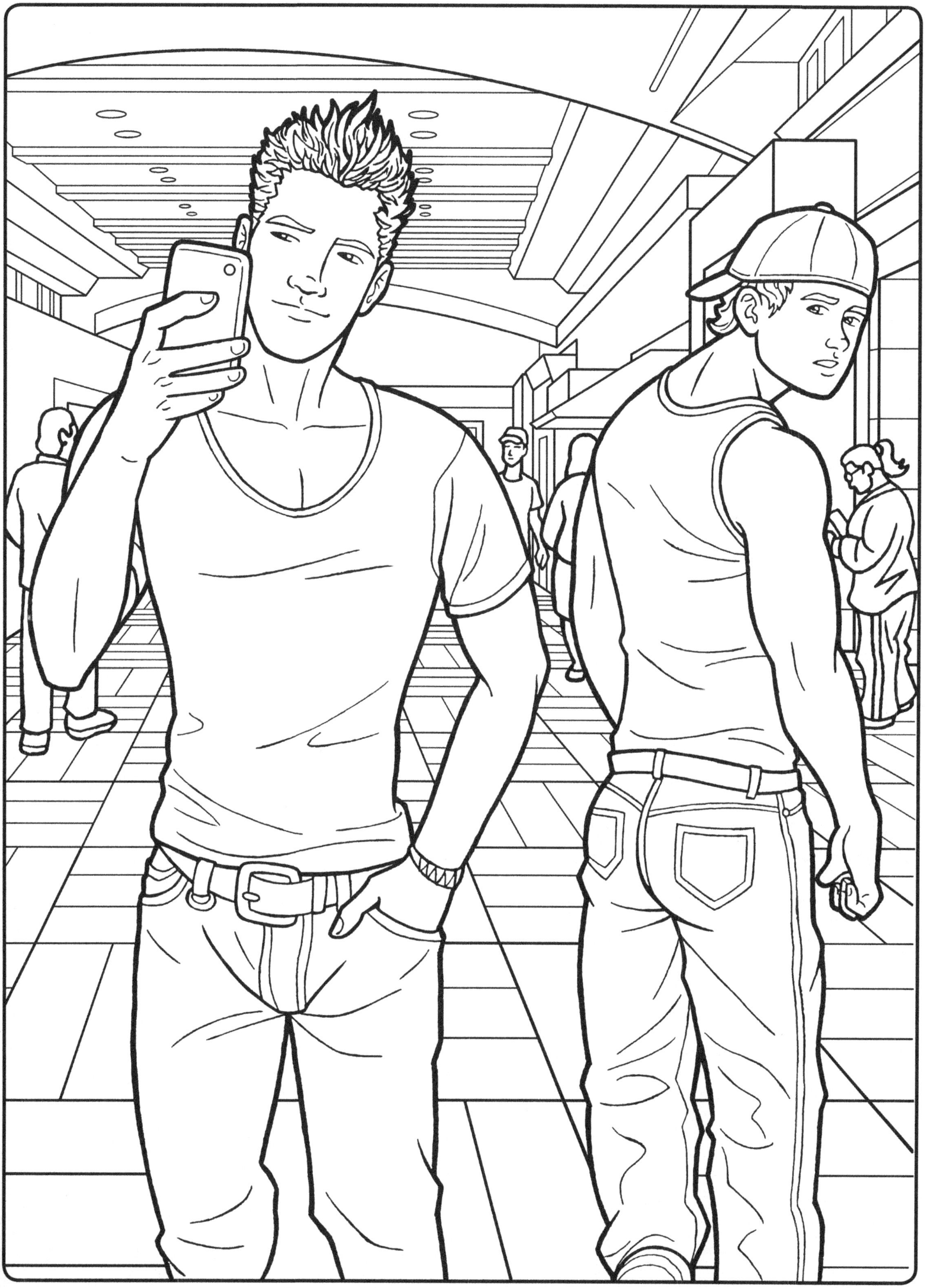

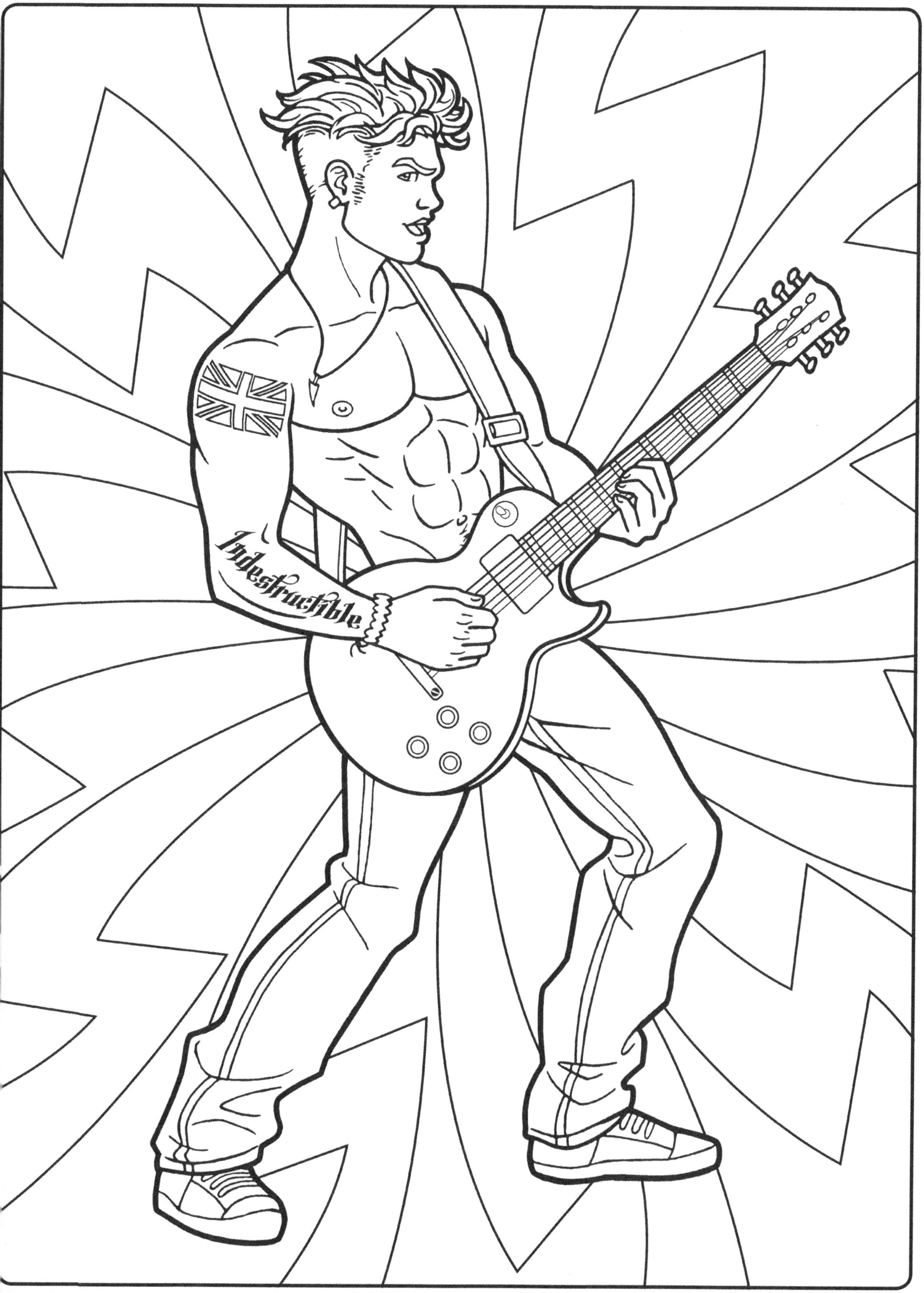
Indestructible

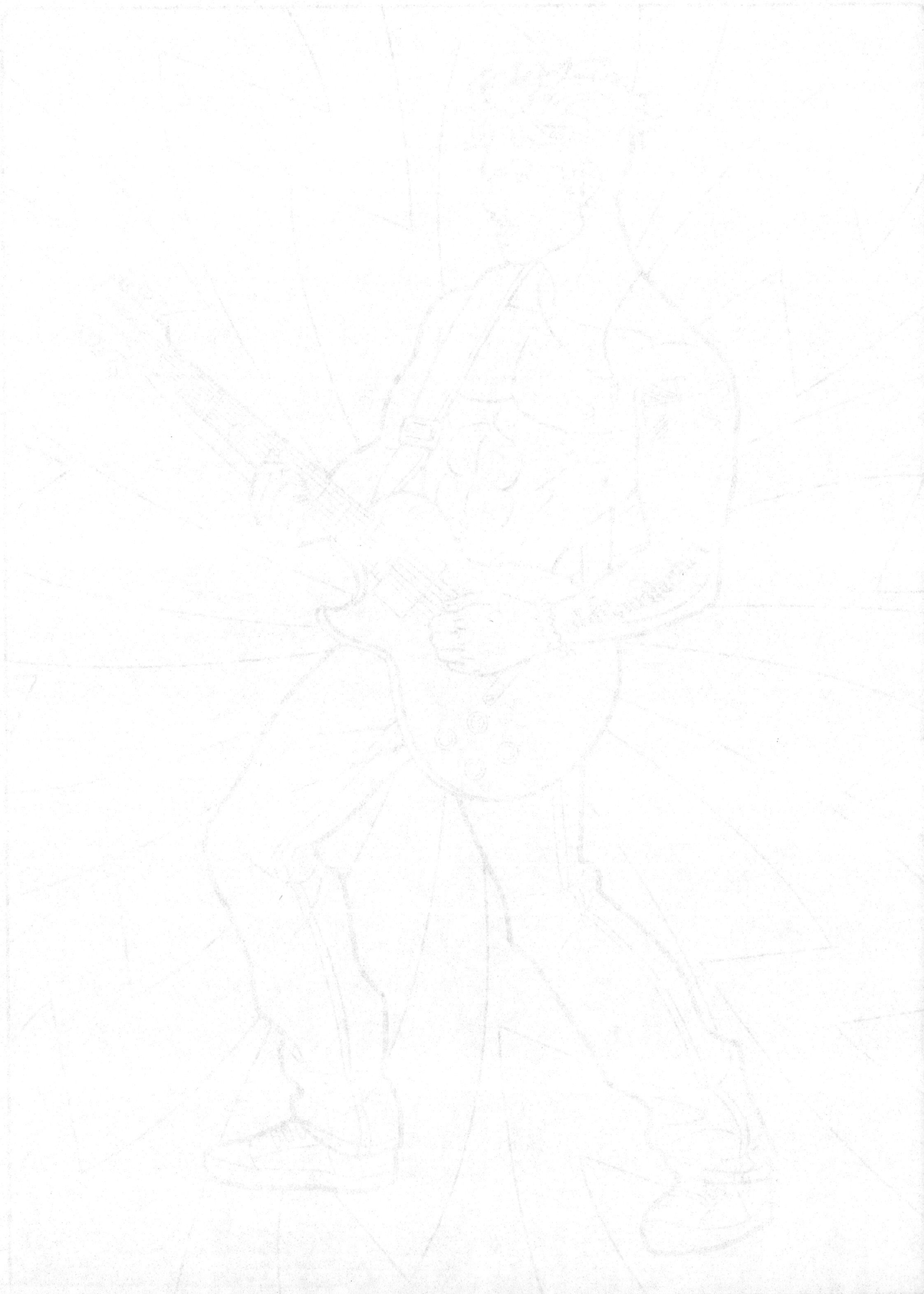

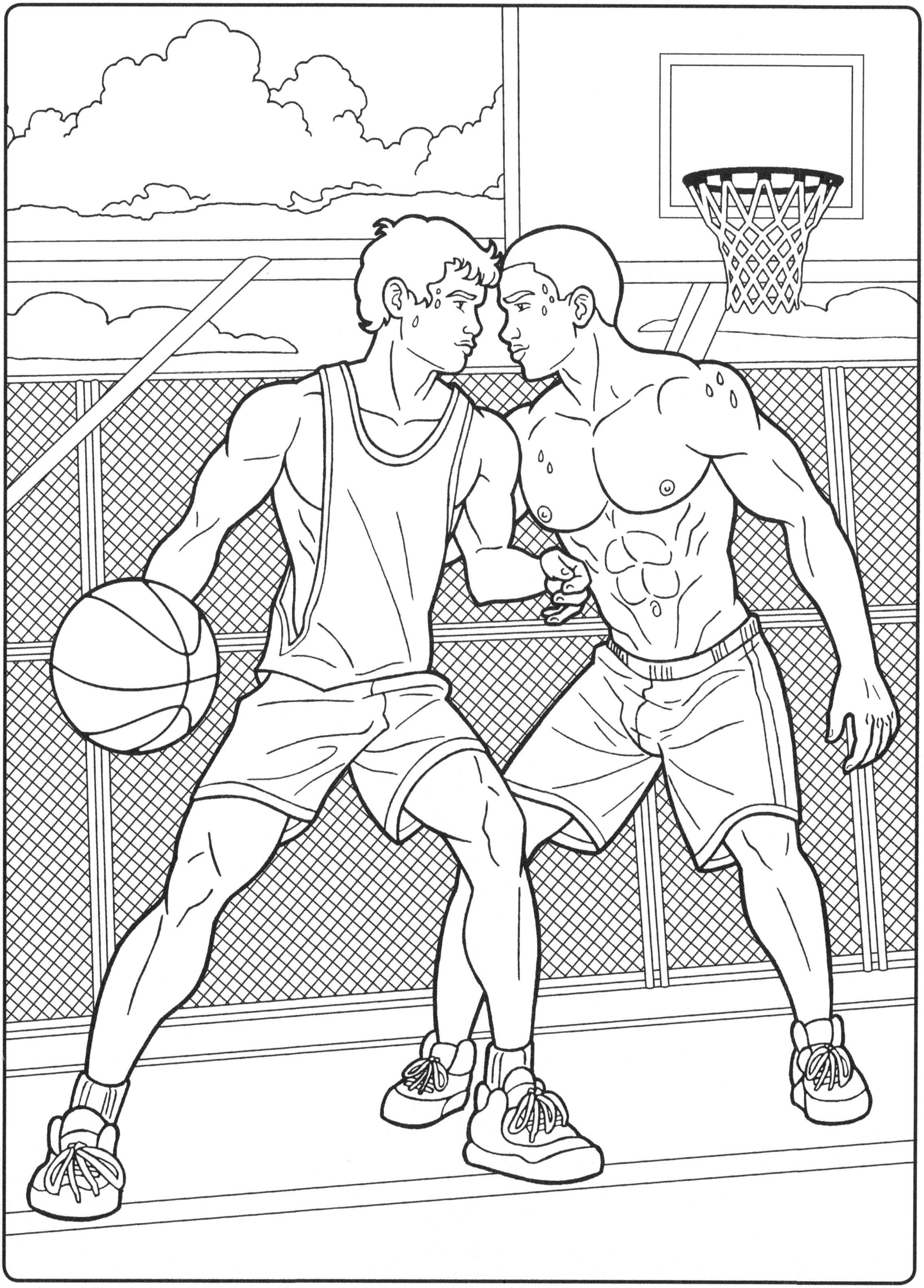

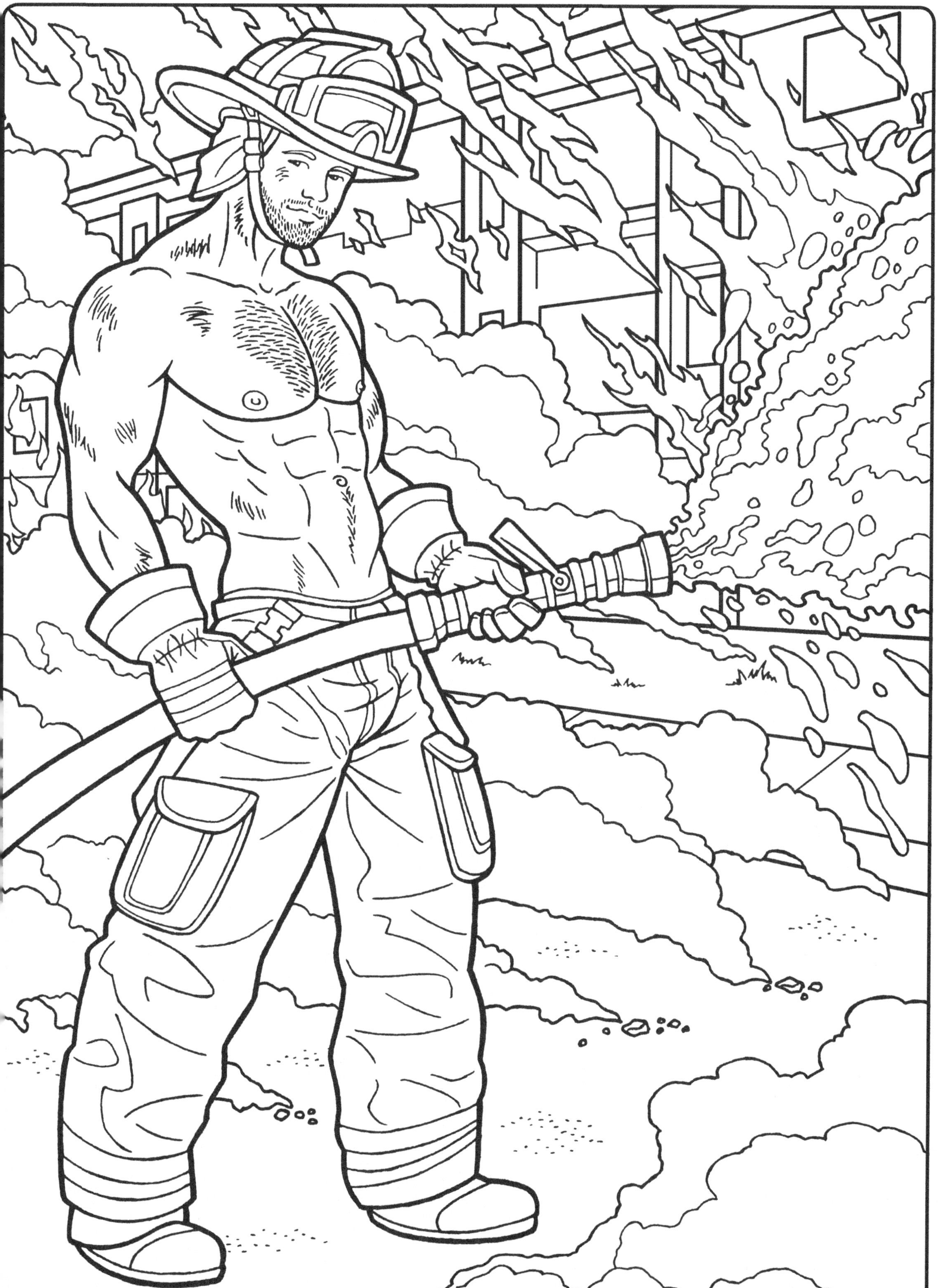

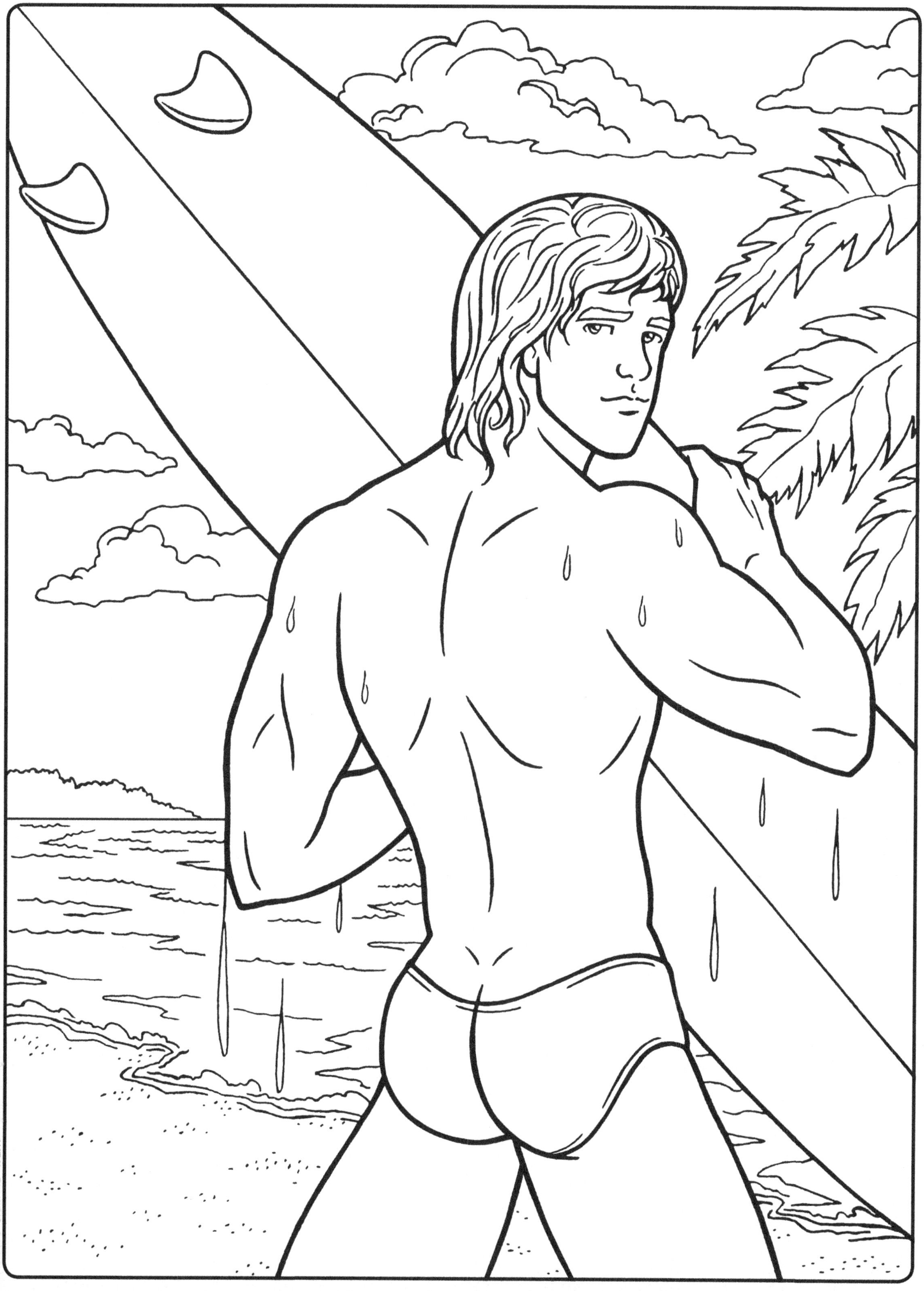

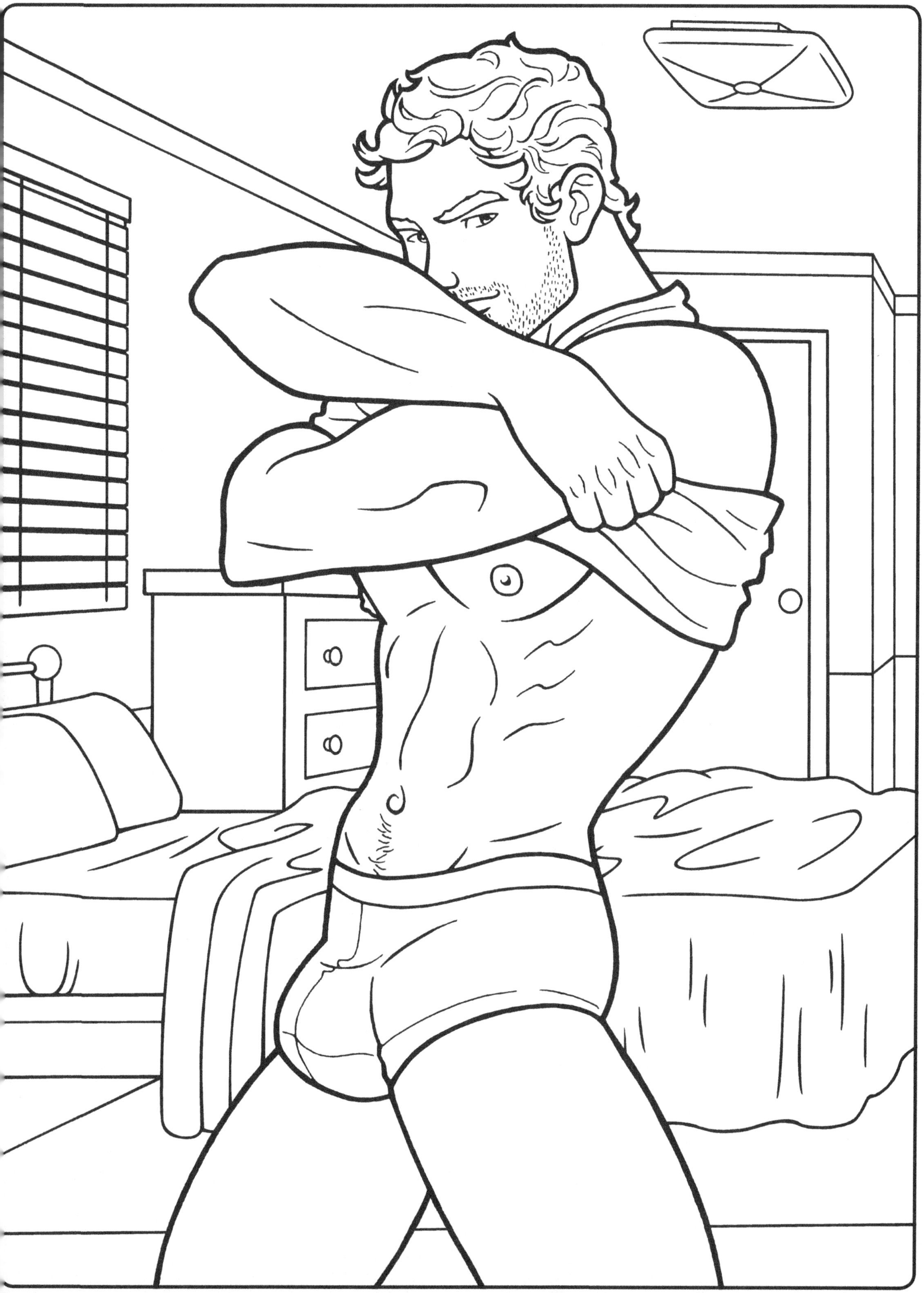

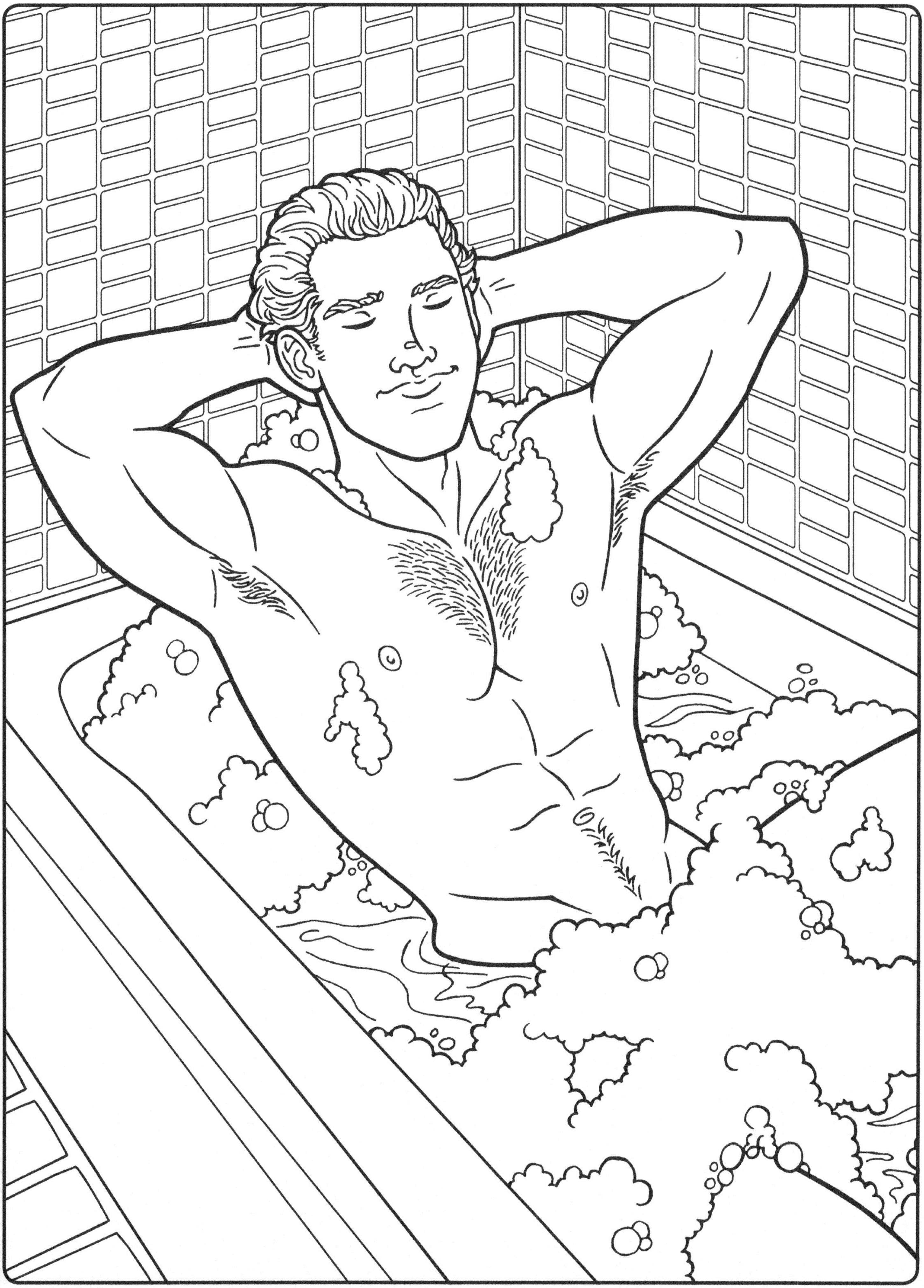

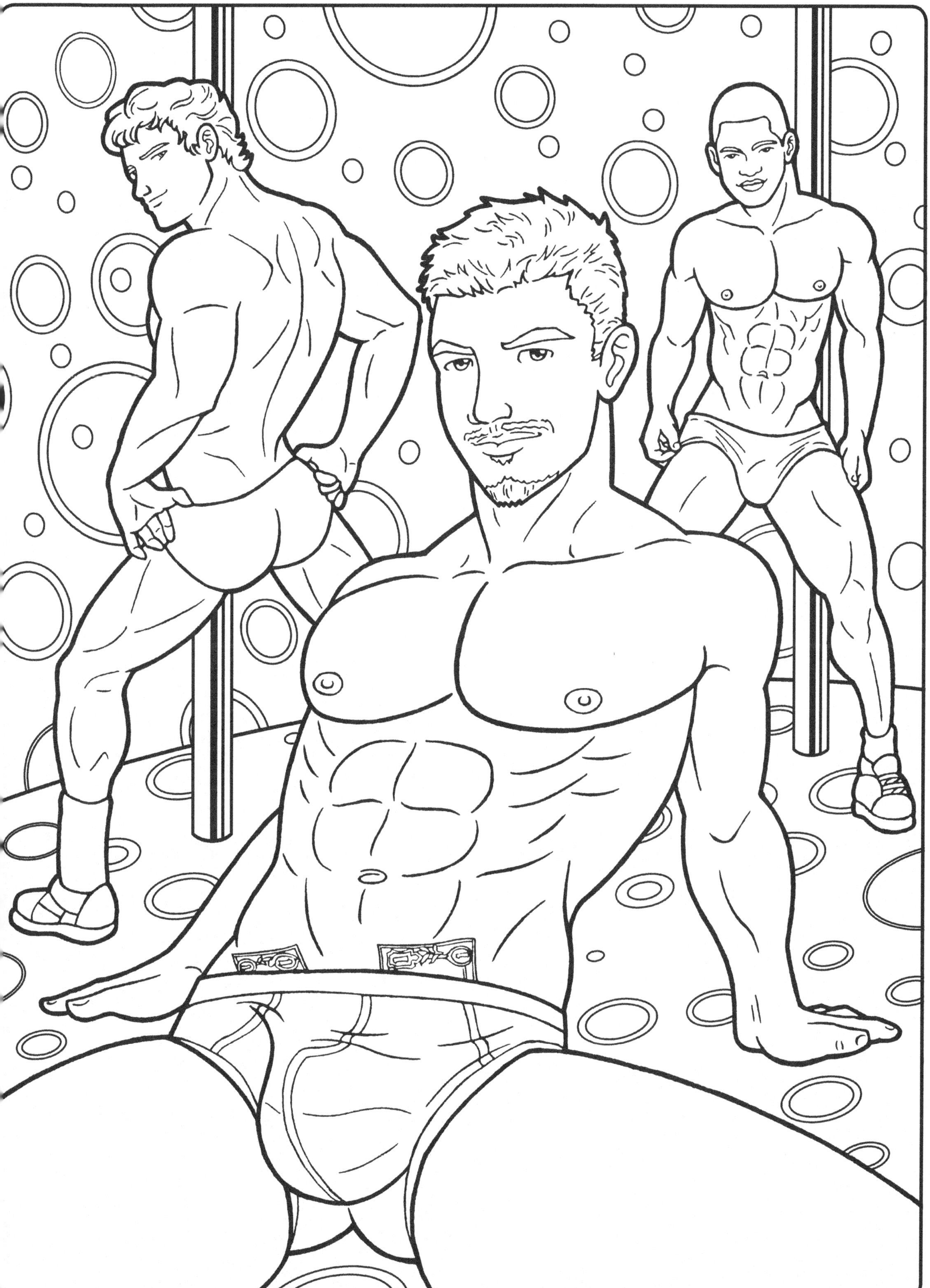

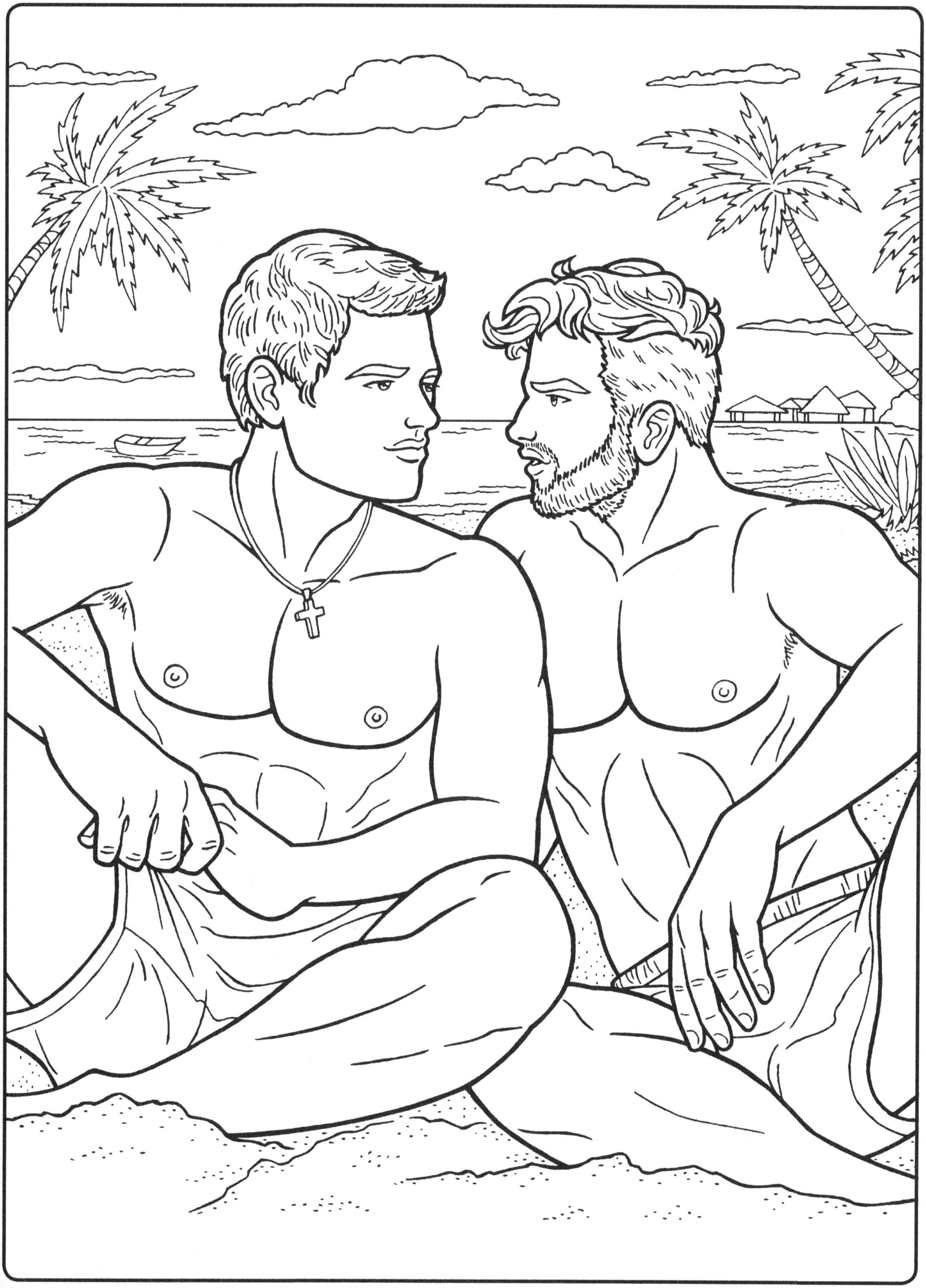

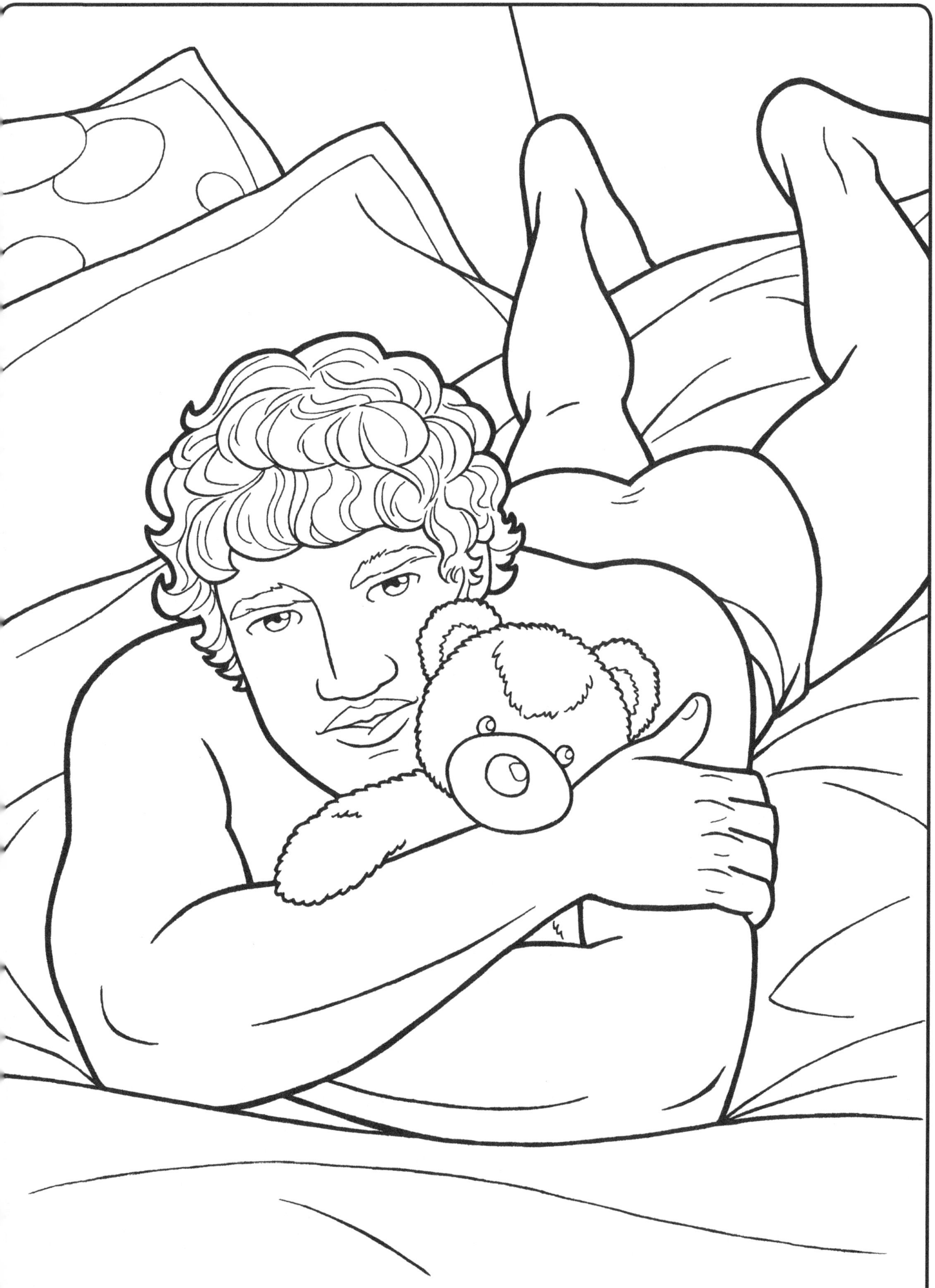

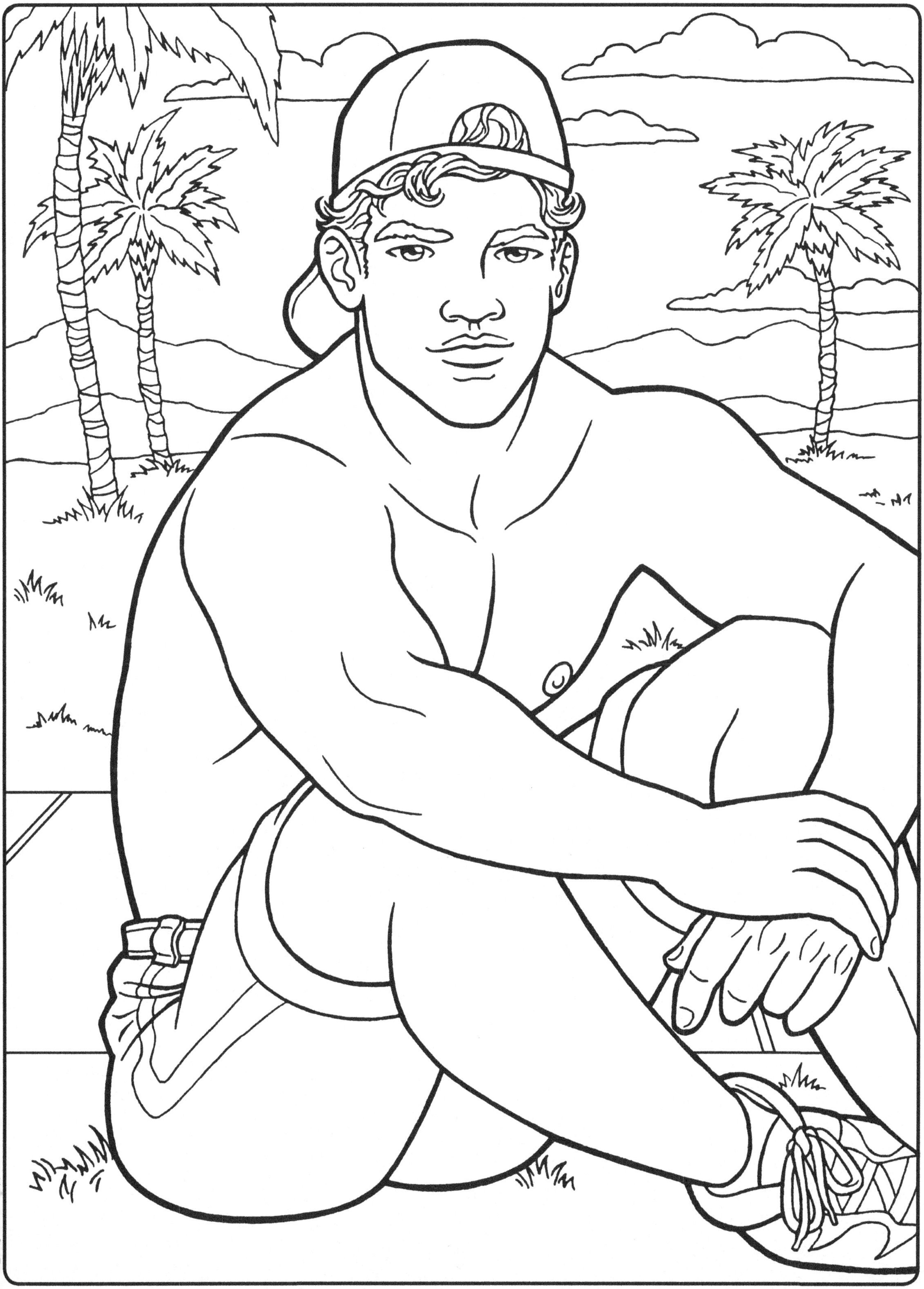

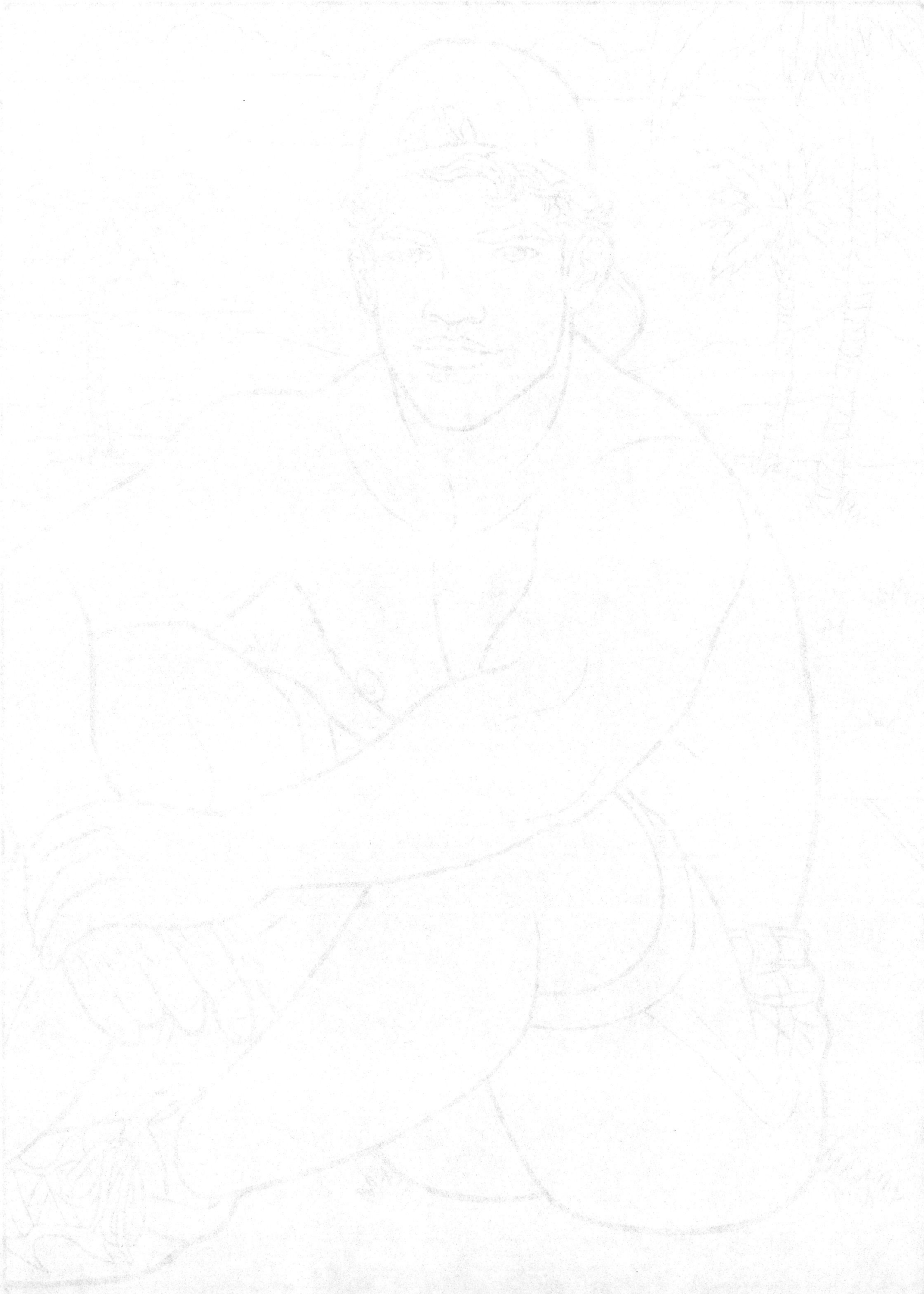

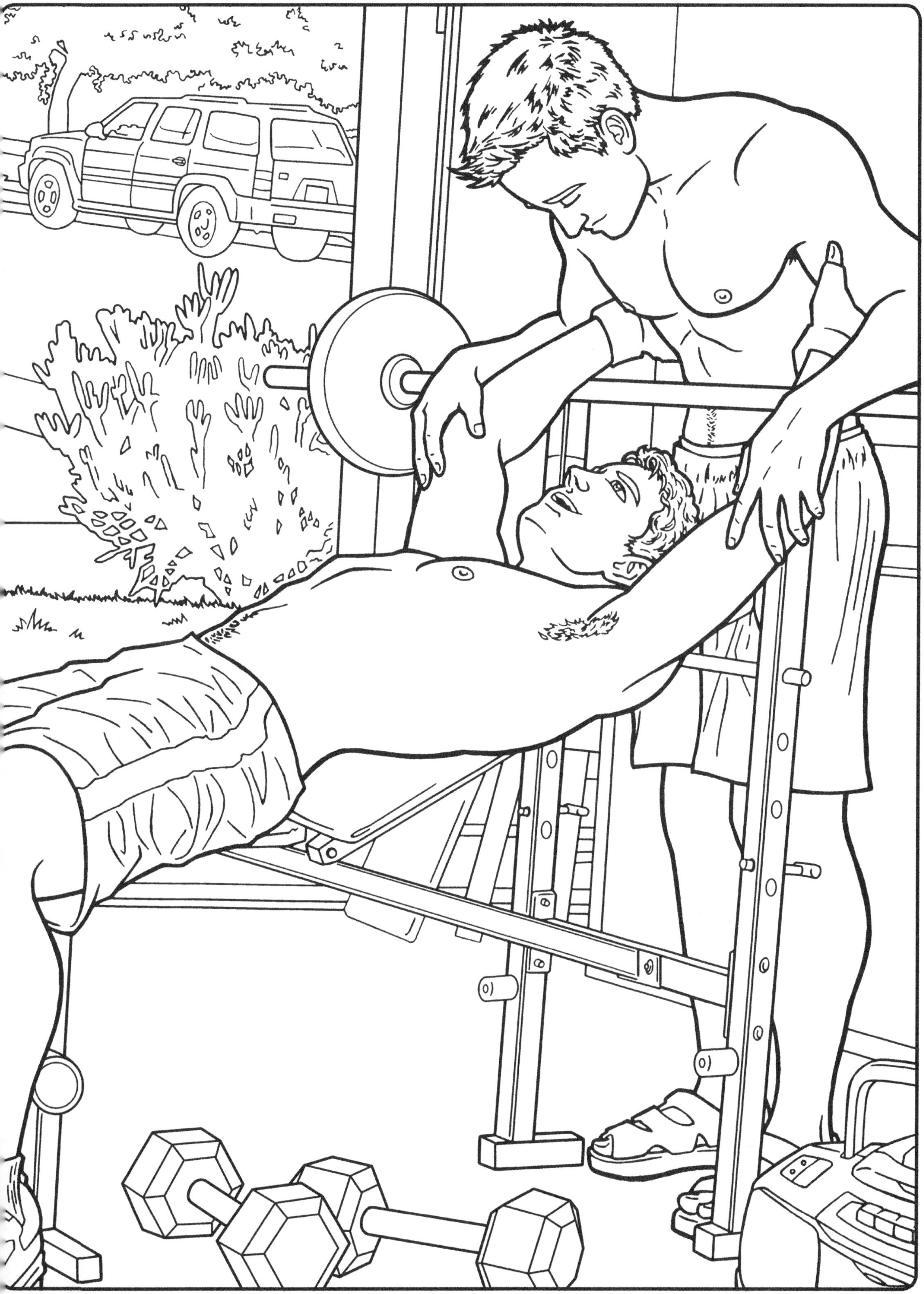

Made in the USA
Las Vegas, NV
11 November 2024

11624551R00031